CHURCHILL

THE WALK WITH DESTINY

CHURCHILL

THE WALK WITH DESTINY

COMPILED AND DESIGNED BY

H. TATLOCK MILLER

LOUDON SAINTHILL

HUTCHINSON OF LONDON

CONTENTS

YOU HAVE BEEN

SO FAITHFUL AND SO LOVING TO US

YOU HAVE

FOUGHT SO STOUTLY FOR US

YOU HAVE BEEN SO

HEARTY IN COUNSELLING OF US

THAT WE SHALL

NEVER FORGET YOUR FAVOUR

TOWARDS US

This quotation from Bunyan's *Pilgrim's Progress* formed
the peroration of the Address by the Elected Members
of the House of Commons to Sir Winston Churchill on the
occasion of his Eightieth Birthday, November 30th, 1954

The Arms of Sir Winston L. Spencer Churchill, K.G., O.M., C.H., M.P., Prime Minister

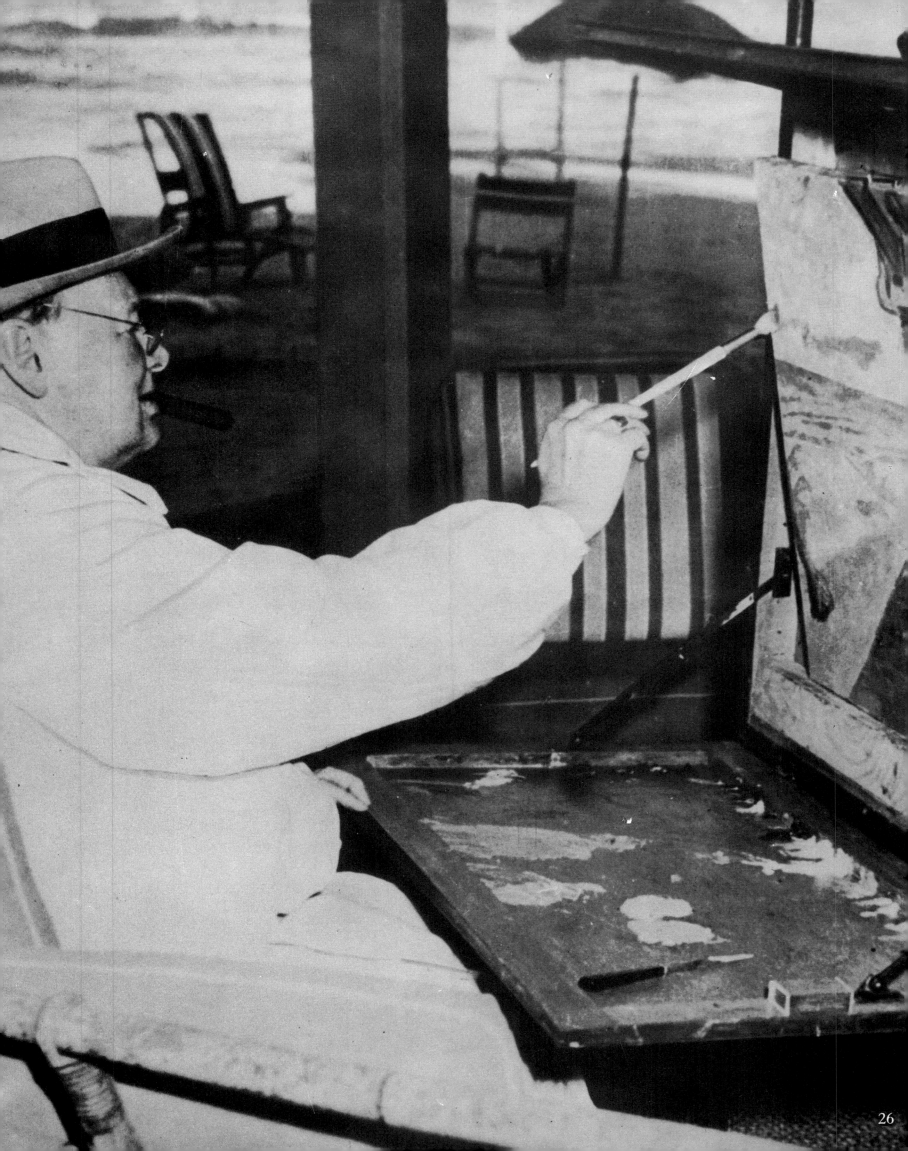

ROYAL ACADEMY OF ARTS.

TOMBEAU
DE
MALBOROUK

IN THE BEGINNING

'*Another Churchill joined the line to*
stand where Marlborough had stood, when
a fresh challenge sounded . . .'

PHILIP GUEDALLA

UNDER THE AUSPICES OF A MUNIFICENT SOVEREIGN THIS HOUSE
WAS BUILT FOR JOHN DUKE OF MARLBOROUGH, AND HIS DUCHESS
SARAH, BY SIR J. VANBRUGH BETWEEN THE YEARS 1705 AND 1722.
AND THIS ROYAL MANOR OF WOODSTOCK, TOGETHER WITH A
GRANT OF £240.000, TOWARDS THE BUILDING OF BLENHEIM
WAS GIVEN BY HER MAJESTY QUEEN ANNE AND CONFIRMED
BY ACT OF PARLIAMENT (3. & 4. ANNE C. 4.) TO THE SAID JOHN
DUKE OF MARLBOROUGH AND TO ALL HIS ISSUE MALE AND
FEMALE LINEALLY DESCENDING.

33

37

The Arms of John, 1st Duke of Marlborough, K.G.

VICTORIAN

'This was the British Antonine Age.
Those who were its children could not understand
why it had not begun earlier or why
it should ever stop.'

SIR WINSTON CHURCHILL

◀ QUEEN VICTORIA, 1854

London, 1865

His paternal grandfather, the 7th Duke of Marlborough (1822-1883), Lord President of the Council and Viceroy of Ireland during Mr. Disraeli's administration.

His father, Lord Randolph
Churchill (1849-1895), third
son of the 7th Duke of
Marlborough, as a young man

His father, Lord Randolph Churchill, had a brilliant career, becoming at the age of thirty-six leader of the House of Commons and Chancellor of the Exchequer in Lord Salisbury's Government.

His mother, Lady Randolph Churchill

BIRTHS.

On the 30th Nov., at Blenheim Palace, the Lady RANDOLPH CHURCHILL, prematurely, of a son.

On the 7th Oct., at Rangoon, the wife of HALKETT F. JACKSON, Esq., Lieut. and Adjutant 67th Regt., of a daughter.

On the 20th Oct., at Bombay, the wife of Capt. G. W. OLDHAM, R.E., of a son.

On the 27th Oct., at Ranchi, Chota Nagpore, the wife of Capt. NINIAN LOWIS, B.S.C., Assistant Commissioner, of a daughter.

On the 6th Nov., 1874, at Belgaum, India, the wife of J. CHARLES M. PIGOTT, Esq., Lieut. 66th Regt., of a daughter.

On the 20th Nov., at Marlborough-terrace, Roath, Cardiff, the wife of THOMAS J. ALLEN, of a daughter.

On the 21st Nov., the wife of POYNTZ WRIGHT, M.R.C.S.E., of a daughter.

On the 22d Nov., at South-hill-park, Hampstead, the wife of ALBERT STRAUBE, of a son.

On the 26th Nov., at Wolfang, Queensland, Australia, the wife of HENRY DE SATGÉ, Esq., of a son.

On the 27th Nov., at Wolverton House, Bucks, the wife of SPENCER R. HARRISON, Esq., of a daughter.

On the 28th Nov., at Eton College, the wife of ARTHUR C. JAMES, Esq., of a daughter.

On the 28th Nov., at Churt Vicarage, near Farnham, the wife of the Rev. A. B. ALEXANDER, of a daughter.

On the 29th Nov., at 31, Spencer-square, Ramsgate, the wife of Mr. GEO. HAWKINS, late of Brighton, of a son.

On the 29th Nov., at Kibworth Beauchamp, Leicestershire, the wife of THOMAS MACAULAY, Surgeon, of a daughter.

On the 29th Nov., at Nunthorpe Grove, York, Mrs. WOOD CLARKE, of a son.

THE TIMES
DEC. 1, 1874

Blenheim Palace. Seat of the
Dukes of Marlborough

◀ The Gardens, Blenheim Palace

The room at Blenheim in which
Winston Churchill was born

Curls of the infant Churchill
preserved at Blenheim

My dear mama
am so glad
you are coming
o see us I had
uch a nice
athe in the
ea to day.

His first letter.

Winston Churchill with his mother.

' My mother made a brilliant impression upon my childhood's life.
She shone for me like the evening star — I loved her dearly, but at a distance.'

Aged seven, 1881.

Lady Randolph Churchill ▶

62

HARROW, 1889. '. . . this interlude of school makes a sombre grey patch upon the chart of my journey. I am all for the Public Schools but I do not want to go there again.'

SANDHURST, 1894. 'It took me three tries to pass into Sandhurst.' With two friends at the Royal Military Academy just before leaving to be commissioned in the 4th Queen's Hussars.

A subaltern, 1895, in the full dress uniform of the regiment. In March, two months after the death of his father, Lord Randolph, he was gazetted to the 4th Hussars. 'I joined the Regiment six weeks earlier in anticipation, and was immediately set with several other subalterns to the stiff and arduous training of a Recruit Officer.'

INDIA, 1896.   Stationed at Bangalore with the 4th Hussars.   A keen polo player he yet found time and
'resolved to read history, philosophy, economics, and things like that . . . I got out the eight volumes of
Gibbon's DECLINE AND FALL OF THE ROMAN EMPIRE.'

Correspondent to the 'Morning Post' South Africa.

1899.　'Twenty to twenty-five !　Those are the years !'　His political career began when he stood as the Conservative candidate in Oldham and made his first political speech at Bath after seeing active service in India and commanding a troop of the 21st Lancers in the charge of the Battle of Omdurman in the Sudan.

Lady Randolph
Churchill as the
Empress Theodora.

£25.—.—

(vijf en twintig pond stg.)
belooning uitgeloofd door
de Sub-Commissie van Wijk V
voor den Specialen Constabel
dezer wijk, die den ontvluchte
Krijgsgevangene
Churchill
levend of dood te dezer kantore
aflevert.—

Namens de Sub-Comm.
Wijk V
de Haas
Sec

Translation.

£25

(Twenty-five Pounds stg.) REWARD is offered by the Sub-Commission of the fifth division, on behalf of the Special Constable of the said division, to anyone who brings the escaped prisioner of war

CHURCHILL,

dead or alive to this office.

For the Sub-Commission of the fifth division.
(Signed) LODK. de HAAS Sec.

BOER WAR.   War correspondent of the 'Morning Post.' He was taken prisoner by Botha but escaped from Pretoria within one month, becoming a world-famous figure overnight.

PRISONER OF WAR, 1899. The Boers 'were the most good-hearted enemy I have ever fought against in the four continents in which it has been my fortune to see active service.'

He was commisioned in the South African Light Horse. His book, '*The River War*' was published; also '*Savrola*' his only novel. 'I have consistently urged my friends to abstain from reading it.'

After his spectacular escape from the Boers, his reception at Durban was rapturous. He speaks at the Town Hall. He returned to England after taking part in the relief of Ladysmith and the capture of Johannesburg, and at the 'Khaki' election of 1900 was elected member for Oldham.

The Relief of Ladysmith. London celebrates outside the Mansion House.

The funeral procession of Her Majesty Queen Victoria, 1901.

'The fifteenth Parliament of Queen Victoria
would be meeting in the first
weeks of 1901. But before it could
assemble, an old lady faded out
of life at Osborne; and the new member for
Oldham found himself in the first
Parliament of King Edward VII.'

PHILIP GUEDALLA

Coronation Day, London, 1902.

' THE EDWARDIAN AGE was by no means a mere
retarded echo of the Victorian. Its character was
all its own, though (like the sovereign from whom
it took its name) it was denied its full expression
by the force of circumstances until rather late
in life. Its patriotism, which had survived the
challenge of events in Ireland and more recently
in South Africa, was for that reason less
instinctive and unquestioning than its predecessor's.
It could recite the reasons for its British faith,
because it had been forced to find out what
they were ; and a more reasoned loyalty found an
expression that was more conscious in the same
measure as the swelling note of Elgar's Land
of Hope and Glory ' (composed for King Edward's
Coronation) exceeded the artless airs of
patriotic music in the reign of Queen Victoria.
Was the note a little forced ? Perhaps there
was a growing sense that there were other countries
in the world and that British voices must be
raised a little, if they were to prevail. For it
was an age of widening apprehension . . .'

PHILIP GUEDALLA

King Edward VII.

He made his maiden speech ('. . . the Boers who are fighting in the field—and if I were a Boer I hope I should be fighting in the field . . .') in 1901. He crossed the floor of the House to join the Liberal benches in disagreement with Chamberlain's policy of protection in 1904.

FIRST OFFICE. In 1906 he became Under-Secretary of State for the Colonies in Campbell-Bannerman's Ministry, and the following year was sworn a Privy Councillor. 'Lord Randolph Churchill' was published.

Winston Spencer Churchill

Ogden's *Guinea Gold Cigarettes.*

At the age of 33 he was appointed President of the Board of Trade and entered the Cabinet in 1908. (' I've got this pie too late ; L.G. has pulled out all the plums.').

He became engaged to Miss Clementine Hosier in 1908. ' I married and lived happily ever afterwards.'

was married at St. Margaret's

urch on September 12th, 1908

With the Kaiser, German Army manoeuvres, 1909.

He was appointed Home Secretary in 1910. He walks to the House of Commons on Budget Day with Mr. Lloyd George, the Chancellor of the Exchequer, who carries Mr. Gladstone's despatch box.

Mr. and Mrs. Churchill, 1910.

Mrs. Churchill
at Ranelagh.

Pheasant Shoot,
Yorkshire.

Mr. and Mrs. Churchill with General Bruce Hamilton during British Army Manoeuvres at Aldershot in the Summer of 1910.

On the death of King Edward VII, Mr. Churchill, with his cousin, the Duke of Marlborough, called at Buckingham Palace. May 6th, 1910.

Winston Churchill at the Siege of Sydney Street.

Witness at the Sydney Street inquiry.

GEORGIAN

'Just thirty-five, a Secretary of State, a happy husband
and a father, Mr. Churchill occupied an enviable
situation in the first months of 1910.
Sharing with Lloyd George the leadership of the
progressive Liberals, he seemed to be in line
for even greater eminence. After all, Mr. Asquith
could not live for ever; and somebody would
have to be Prime Minister . . .
An added duty was his daily letter to the King
reporting the proceedings of the House of Commons,
and the sovereign enjoyed these spirited effusions. But soon
they were addressed to a new monarch. For King Edward
died that spring, and was succeeded by King George V.'

PHILIP GUEDALLA

Their Majesties, King George V and Queen Mary,
The Royal Procession at the Delhi Durbar.

The First Lord of the Admiralty with his mother, Armada Day, 1912.

Mr. Churchill was attacked by suffragettes some of whom were
arrested after attacking Buckingham Palace on May 31st, 1914.

108

Walking along Whitehall to a Cabinet meeting at 10 Downing Street.
In July, 1914, he prevented the dispersal of the Home Fleet.

He leaves 10 Downing Street after a conference. On his own responsibility he ordered mobilisation of the Fleet on August the first. Two days later he was able to say : ' The entire Navy is now on a war footing.'

No-man's land.
Passchendaele.

Men of the 9th East Yorks going up to the line.   Near Frazenberg, October 15th, 1917.

Cape Helles. A soldier's grave on the cliff.

Mr. Churchill, an early flying enthusiast, flies over Portsmouth Harbour. He introduced an Air Arm into the Navy.

Soldier in France, 1915.   When the Government decided to abandon the forcing of the Dardanelles, Mr. Churchill resigned from the Government. 'I am finished,' he wrote to Lord Riddell on losing his position at the Admiralty. He joined the Army in France.

He rejoined Mr. Lloyd George's Government as Minister of Munitions in 1917.

'. . . the war was over and the bells began to ring . . .' Armistice Day, London, November 11th, 1918.

Mr. Churchill was appointed Secretary of State for War and for Air, 1919.

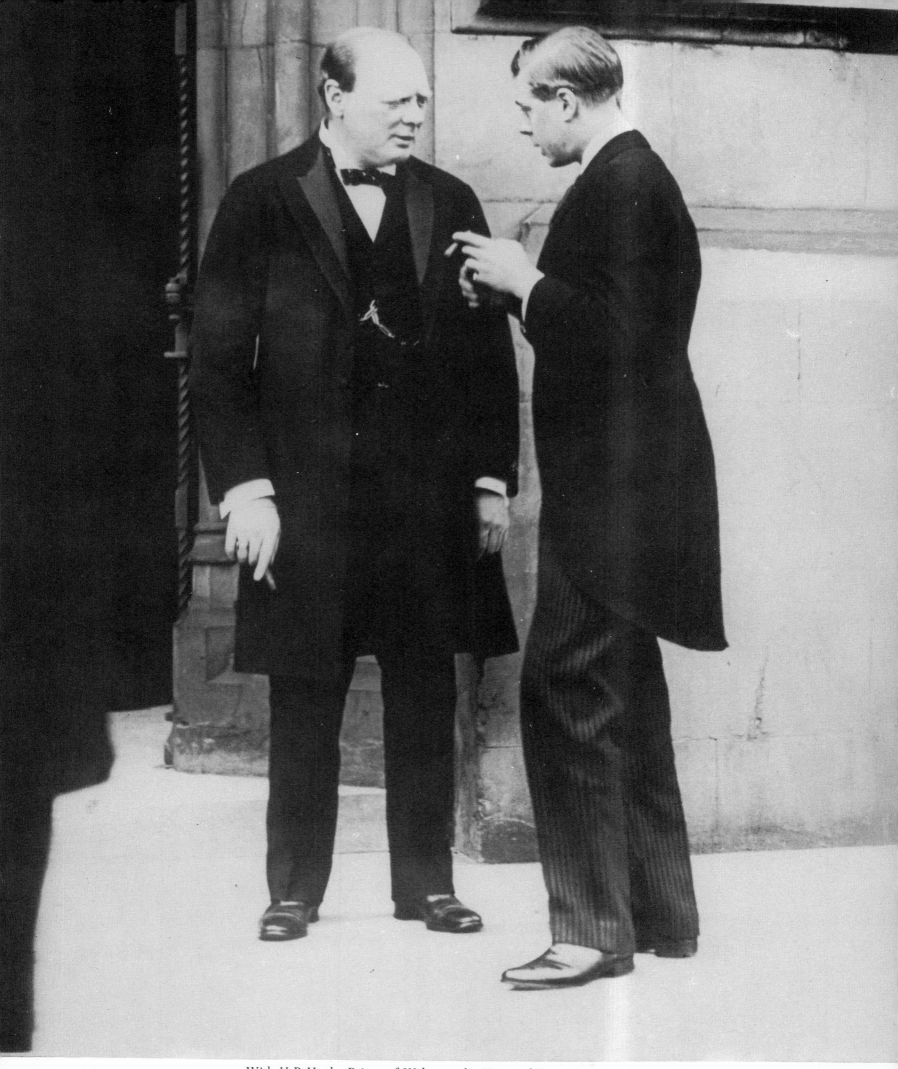

With H.R.H. the Prince of Wales, at the House of Commons, 1919.

THE COLONIAL SECRETARY.

Deauville, August, 1922.   Mrs. Churchill at Beaulieu, 1922. ▶

Polo, 1923.

Mr. and Mrs. Churchill with their daughter Mary, 1924. ▶

130

' I was surprised, and the Conservative Party dumbfounded when he (Mr. Baldwin) invited me to become Chancellor of the Exchequer, the office which my father had once held.'

Deauville, 1927. With the Duke of Sutherland.

Chartwell, 1928. A member of the Amalgamated Union of Building Trades Workers.

Budget Day, 1929.

The Chancellor of the Exchequer, carrying his despatch box, walks with his family to the House of Commons.

California, 1929.

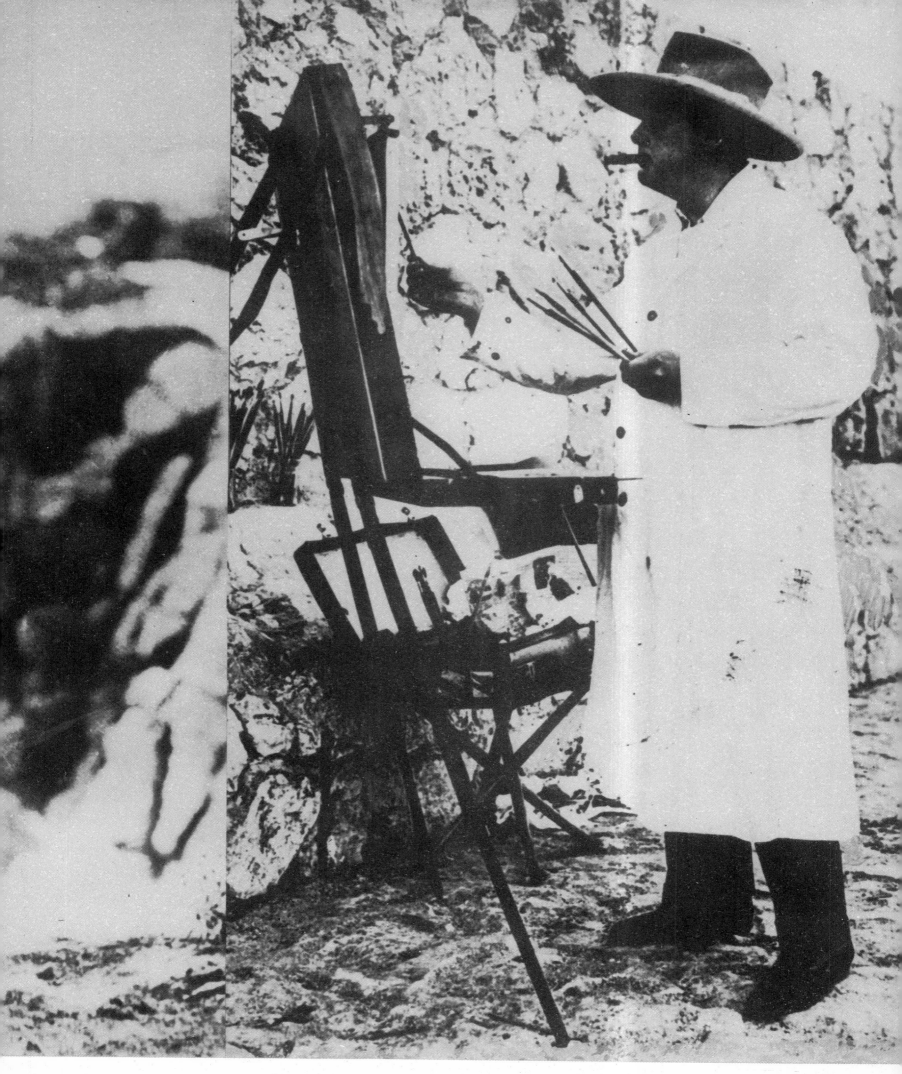

The South of France.

Mr. and Mrs. Churchill with their second daughter, Sarah, at the first court of the Season, 1933.

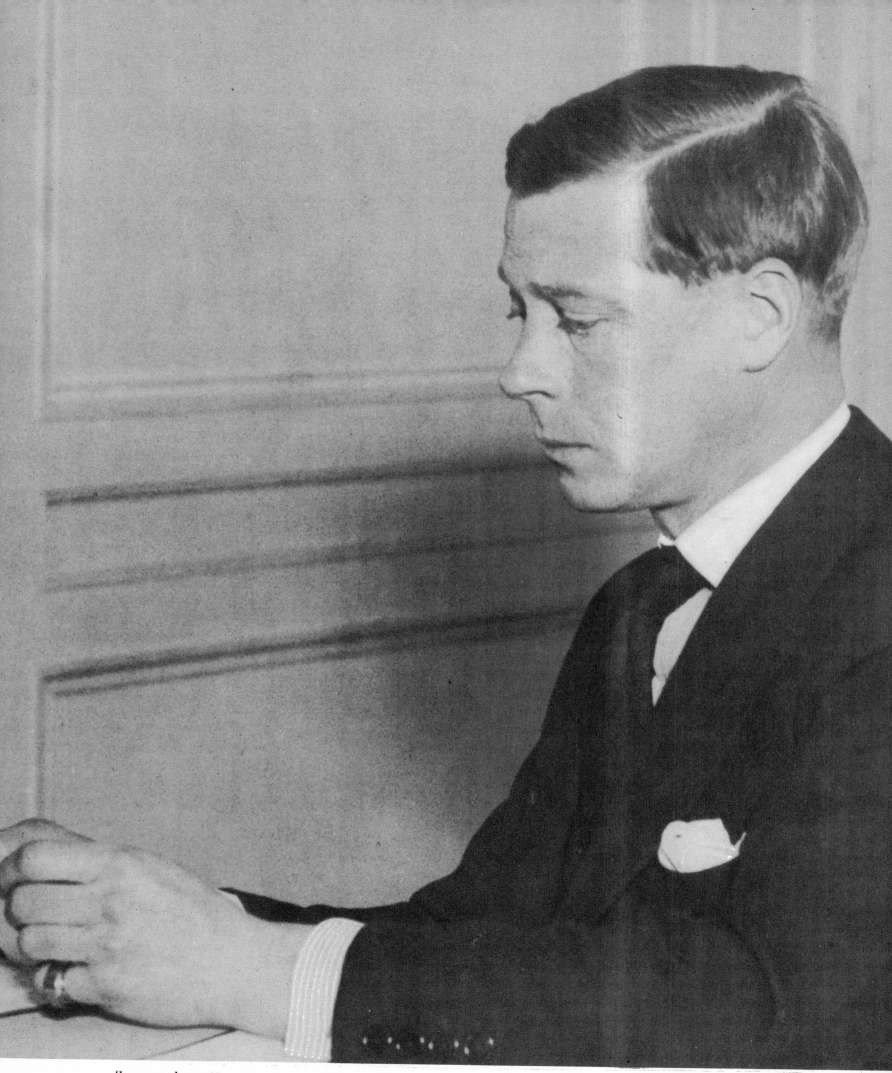

'It was my duty as Home Secretary more than a quarter of a century ago to stand beside His Majesty and proclaim his style and titles at his investiture as Prince of Wales . . . I should have been ashamed if, in my independent and unofficial position I had not cast about for every lawful means, even the most forlorn, to keep him on the Throne of his fathers.'

King Edward VIII abdicated on 11th December, 1936.

' I lived mainly at Chartwell (1931-1935) where I had much to amuse me. I built with my own hands a large part of two
cottages and extensive kitchen-garden walls, and made all kinds of rockeries and waterworks . . . Thus I never had a dull
or idle moment from morning till midnight . . . '

143

Chartwell. 'I have been a journalist half my lifetime and I
have earned my living by selling words and I hope thoughts.'

' . . . in 1900 . . . I could boast to have written as many books as Moses, and I have
not stopped writing them since, except when momentarily interrupted by war . . .

Mr. Neville Chamberlain returns with the Peace Treaty from Munich. '. . . His all-pervading hope was to go down to history as the Great Peacemaker ; and for this he was prepared to strive continually in the face of facts, and face great risks for himself and his country. Unhappily he ran into tides the force of which he could not measure, and met hurricanes from which he did not flinch but with which he could not cope.'

'*There was a terrible simplicity about the order of events . . . that sunny Friday had been chosen by the Germans for the opening of their assault on Western Europe; and as neutral Amsterdam and Brussels heard bombs for the first time, French and British armies moved forward to the rescue, ominously undisturbed by any German bombing. The trap was nicely baited. But the uncanny symmetry of history supplied the antidote in the very instant of administering the poison. For the same evening in London Mr. Churchill was invited by King George to form a Government.*'

PHILIP GUEDALLA

'I felt as if I were walking with destiny'

Germany invaded Poland on the first of September, 1939. Britain mobilised immediately. The Prime Minister, Mr. Chamberlain, asked Mr. Churchill to visit him that afternoon and invited him to become a member of the War Cabinet.

On the third of September Great Britain declared war on Germany. The following day Mr. Churchill returned to the Admiralty as First Lord. The Board of Admiralty signalled to the Fleet the laconic message: 'Winston is back.'

'. . . on the night of the tenth of May (1940) . . .
I acquired the chief power in the State . . . I was conscious of a profound sense of relief.
At last I had the authority to give directions over the whole scene.

I felt as if I were walking with destiny, and that
all my past life had been but a preparation for this hour and for this trial.

Eleven years in the political wilderness
had freed me from ordinary Party antagonisms . . . I thought I knew
a good deal about it all, and I was sure I should not fail.

Therefore, although impatient for the morning
I slept soundly and had no need for cheering dreams.

Facts are better than dreams.'

THE GATHERING STORM, WAR MEMOIRS, VOL. I.

'I was sure I should not fail'

151

He was the voice of England

'and I say,
Come, then, let us go forward'

'I would say to the House, as I said to those who have joined this Government: 'I have nothing to offer but blood, toil, tears and sweat'. We have before us an ordeal of the most grievous kind. We have before us many, many long months of struggle and of suffering. You ask what is our policy? I will say: It is to wage war, by sea, land and air, with all our might and with all the strength that God can give us: to wage war against monstrous tyranny, never surpassed in the dark, lamentable catalogue of human crime. That is our policy. You ask, what is our aim? I can answer in one word: Victory—victory at all costs, victory in spite of all terror, victory, however long and hard the road may be; for without victory, there is no survival. Let that be realised; no survival for the British Empire; no survival for all that the British Empire has stood for, no survival for the urge and impulse of the ages, that mankind will move forward towards its goal. But I take up my task with buoyancy and hope. I feel sure that our cause will not be suffered to fail among men. At this time I feel entitled to claim the aid of all, and I say, Come, then, let us go forward together with our united strength.'

A SPEECH TO THE HOUSE OF COMMONS, 13th MAY, 1940.

'Having received His Majesty's commission, I have formed an administration of men and women of every party and of almost every point of view. We have differed and quarrelled in the past; but now one bond unites us all—to wage war until victory is won, and never to surrender ourselves to servitude and shame whatever the cost and the agony may be. This is one of the most awe-striking periods in the long history of France and Britain. It is also beyond doubt the most sublime. Side by side, unaided except by their kith and kin in the great dominions and by the wide Empires which rest beneath their shield—side by side, the British and French peoples have advanced to rescue not only Europe but mankind from the foulest and most soul-destroying tyranny which has ever darkened and stained the pages of history. Behind them—behind us—behind the armies and fleets of Britain and France—gather a group of shattered States and bludgeoned races; the Czechs, the Poles, the Norwegians, the Danes, the Dutch, the Belgians—upon all of whom the long night of barbarism will descend unbroken even by a star of hope, unless we conquer, as conquer we must; as conquer we shall.'

A WORLD BROADCAST, 19th MAY, 1940.

'Arm yourselves,
and be ye men of valour'

'Today is Trinity Sunday. Centuries ago words were written to be a call and a spur to the faithful servants of truth and justice: 'Arm yourselves, and be ye men of valour, and be in readiness for the conflict; for it is better for us to perish in battle than to look upon the outrage of our nation and our altar. As the Will of God is in Heaven, even so let it be.'

A WORLD BROADCAST, 19th MAY, 1940.

'I have, myself, full confidence that if all do their duty, if nothing is neglected, and if the best arrangements are made, as they are being made, we shall prove ourselves once again able to defend our island home, to ride out the storm of war, and to outlive the menace of tyranny, if necessary for years, if necessary alone. At any rate, that is what we are going to try to do. That is the resolve of His Majesty's Government—every man of them. That is the will of Parliament and the nation . . .

'Even though large tracts of Europe and many old and famous States have fallen or may fall into the grip of the Gestapo and all the odious apparatus of Nazi rule, we shall not flag or fail. We shall go on to the end, we shall fight in France, we shall fight on the seas and oceans, we shall fight with growing confidence and growing strength in the air, we shall defend our island, whatever the cost may be, we shall fight on the beaches, we shall fight on the landing grounds, we shall fight in the fields and in the streets, we shall fight in the hills; we shall never surrender, and even if, which I do not for a moment believe, this island or a large part of it were subjugated and starving, then our Empire beyond the seas, armed and guarded by the British Fleet, would carry on the struggle, until, in God's good time, the new world, with all its power and might, steps forth to the rescue and the liberation of the old.'

A SPEECH TO THE HOUSE OF COMMONS, 4th JUNE, 1940.

'We shall go on to the end'

'We serve an unfolding purpose'

'I expect that the Battle of Britain is about to begin. Upon this battle depends the survival of Christian civilization. Upon it depends our own British life, and the long continuity of our institutions and our Empire. The whole fury and might of the enemy must very soon be turned on us. Hitler knows that he will have to break us in this island or lose the war. If we can stand up to him, all Europe may be free and the life of the world may move forward into broad, sunlit uplands. But if we fail, then the whole world, including the United States, including all that we have known and cared for, will sink into the abyss of a new dark age made more sinister, and perhaps more protracted, by the lights of perverted science. Let us therefore brace ourselves to our duties, and so bear ourselves that, if the British Empire and its Commonwealth last for a thousand years, men will say, 'This was their finest hour'.'

A SPEECH DELIVERED TO THE HOUSE OF COMMONS AND THEN BROADCAST, 18th JUNE, 1940.

'Bearing ourselves humbly before God, but conscious that we serve an unfolding purpose, we are ready to defend our native land against the invasion by which it is threatened. We are fighting by ourselves alone; but we are not fighting for ourselves alone. Here in this strong City of Refuge which enshrines the title-deeds of human progress and is of deep consequence to Christian civilization; here, girt about by the seas and oceans where the Navy reigns; shielded from above by the prowess and devotion of our airmen—we await undismayed the impending assault. Perhaps it will come tonight . . . But be the ordeal sharp or long, or both, we shall seek no terms, we shall tolerate no parley, we may show mercy—we shall ask for none . . . We shall defend every village, every town, and every city.'

'I stand at the head of a Government representing all parties in the State—all creeds, all classes, every recognisable section of opinion. We are ranged beneath the Crown of our ancient Monarchy. We are supported by a free Parliament and a free Press; but there is one bond which unites us all and sustains us in the public regard—namely (as is increasingly becoming known), that we are prepared to proceed to all extremities, to endure them and to enforce them; that is our bond of union in His Majesty's Government tonight. Thus only, in times like these, can nations preserve their freedom; and thus only can they uphold the cause entrusted to their care . . .'

A WORLD BROADCAST, 14th JULY, 1940.

'Long, dark months of trials and tribulations lie before us. Not only great dangers, but many more misfortunes, many shortcomings, many mistakes, many disappointments will surely be our lot. Death and sorrow will be the companions of our journey; hardship our garment; constancy and valour our only shield. We must be united, we must be undaunted, we must be inflexible.'

A SPEECH TO THE HOUSE OF COMMONS, 8th OCTOBER, 1940.

'Our qualities and deeds must burn and glow
through the gloom of Europe until they become
the veritable beacon of its salvation'

'The gratitude of every home in our island, in our Empire, and indeed throughout the world, except in the abodes of the guilty, goes out to the British airmen, who, undaunted by odds, unwearied in their constant challenge and mortal danger, are turning the tide of the world war by their prowess and by their devotion. Never in the field of human conflict was so much owed by so many to so few.'

SPEECH TO THE HOUSE OF COMMONS, AUGUST 20th, 1940

LONDON. The night of
December 29th, 1940.
The City seen from
the Dome of St. Pauls.

'Hitler has lighted a fire
which will burn with a
steady and consuming
flame until the last
vestiges of Nazi tyranny
have been burnt
out of Europe . . .'

Monday Morning, December 31st, 1940.

'These cruel, wanton, indiscriminate bombings of London are, of course, a part of
Hitler's invasion plans. He hopes, by killing large numbers of civilians, and women and
children, that he will terrorize and cow the people of this mighty imperial city . . .'

The collapse of No. 23 Victoria Street, London, 1940.

The House of Commons was destroyed by ▶
bombs on the night of May 10th, 1941.

'What he has done is to kindle a fire in British hearts, here and all over the world, which will glow long after all traces of the conflagration he has caused in London have been removed. He has lighted a fire which will burn with a steady and consuming flame until the last vestiges of Nazi tyranny have been burnt out of Europe, and until the Old World—and the New—can join hands to rebuild the temples of man's freedom and man's honour, upon foundations which will not soon or easily be overthrown.

' we shall rather draw from the heart of suffering itself the means of inspiration and survival, and of a victory won not only for our own time, but for the long and better days that are to come.'

FROM A BROADCAST SPEECH, SEPTEMBER 11th, 1940.

◀ Westminster Hall and the statue of Richard the First, September 27th, 1940.

On board H.M.S. The Prince of Wales.

'I thought you would like me to tell you something about the voyage which I made across the ocean to meet our great friend, the President of the United States. Exactly where we met is a secret, but I don't think I shall be indiscreet if I go so far as to say that it was 'somewhere in the Atlantic'.'

The Prime Minister and President Roosevelt meet in mid-Atlantic, August, 1941.

'The meeting was . . . symbolic. That is its prime importance. It symbolizes, in a form and manner which everyone can understand in every land and in every clime, the deep underlying unities which stir and at decisive moments rule the English-speaking peoples throughout the world.'

Teheran, November 1943.
Mr. Churchill with President Roosevelt
and Marshall Stalin.

'This was a memorable occasion in
my life. Together we controlled a large
preponderance of the naval and three-
quarters of all the air forces in the world,
and could direct armies of nearly twenty
millions of men, engaged in the most
terrible of wars that had yet occurred in
human history.'

'. . . and . . . after the war when a man is asked what he did it will be quite
sufficient for him to say, 'I marched and fought with the Desert Army.'

'And when history is written and all the facts are known your feats will gleam and glow and will be a source of song and story long after we who are gathered here have passed away.'

Cairo. The Prime Minister with Field Marshal Smuts, the South African
Prime Minister and Sir Arthur Tedder and Sir Alan Brooke, 1942.

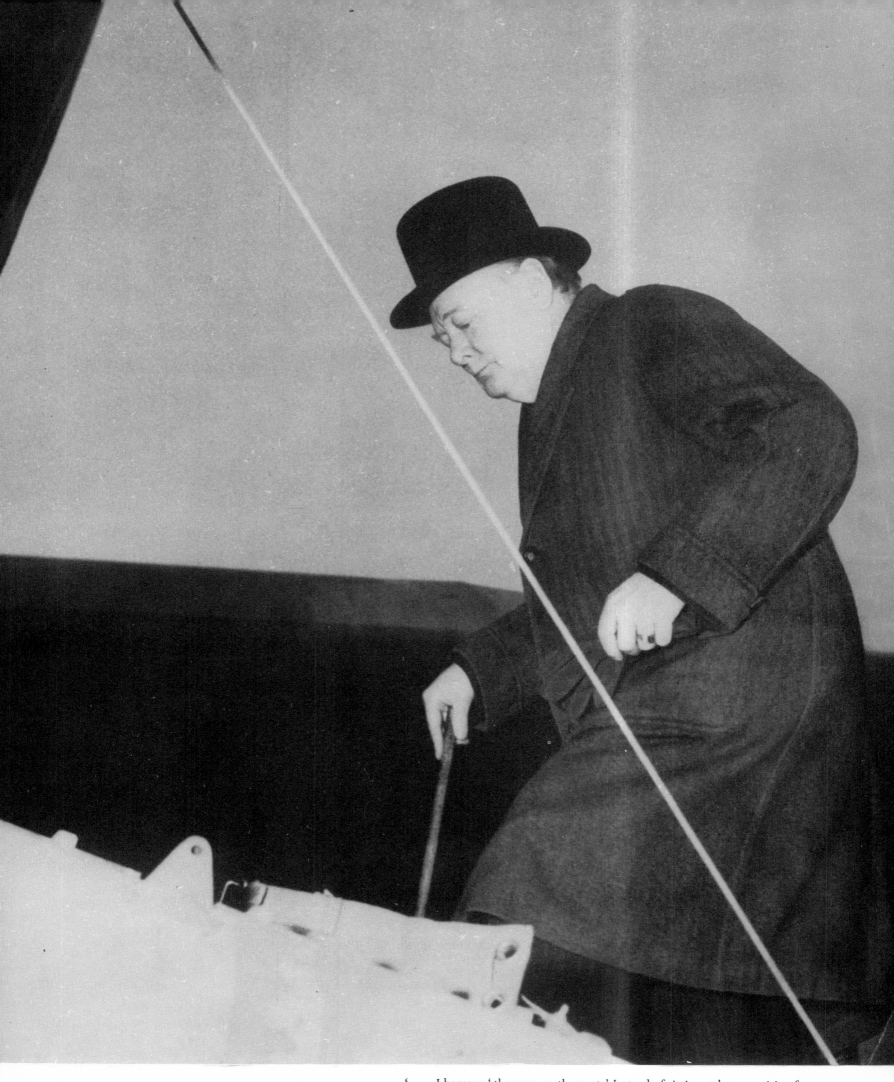

' . . . I became 'the man on the spot.' Instead of sitting at home waiting for
the news from the front I could send it myself. This was exhilarating.'

A flying bomb falling near Drury Lane, London.

'They never flinched or failed . . . Let us give them our salute.' ▶

The Landing in Normandy

'. . . during the night and the early hours of this morning the first of the series of landings in force upon the European continent has taken place. In this case the liberating assault fell upon the coast of France. An immense armada of upwards of 4,000 ships, together with several thousand smaller craft, crossed the Channel. . . . These landings took place with extremely little loss and with great accuracy. Particular anxiety attached to them, because the conditions of light prevailing in the very limited period of the dawn — just before the dawn — the conditions of visibility made all the difference.'

A STATEMENT TO THE HOUSE OF COMMONS, 8th JUNE, 1944.

Tripoli. Reviewing the victorious Eighth Army with General
Montgomery and Lt.-Gen. Sir Oliver Leese, February 8th, 1943.

180

Near Florence, in a forward observation post, Mr. Churchill watches a British Army artillery shoot, August 20th, 1944.

Athens. Mr. Churchill with the Greek Regent, Archbishop Damaskinos, 1944.

Paris, November 10th, 1944. 'We proceeded through wildly cheering multitudes to the Arc de Triomphe . . .'
Paris had been liberated and the Prime Minister walked down the Champs Elysees with General de Gaulle.

The Three-Power Conference at Yalta, February, 1945. 'Sombre indeed would be the fortunes of mankind if some awful situation arose between the Western democracies and the Soviet Union—if the future world organization were rent assunder and a new cataclysm of inconceivable violence destroyed all that is left of the treasures and liberties of mankind.'

FROM A SPEECH TO THE HOUSE OF COMMONS ON THE YALTA CONFERENCE.

The Rhine Front, March, 1945.

Mr. Churchill crossed the Rhine two days after the armies. ' So I said to Montgomery, ' Why don't we go across and have a look at the other side ?'   Somewhat to my surprise he answered, 'Why not ?'.

Germany, March, 1945.
A visit to the Citadel in Julich.

The entrance to the Citadel in Julich. The Prime Minister with
General Montgomery and General Simpson at the 9th Army Front. ▶

' Dragons teeth ' of the captured Siegfried Line on the road to Aachen.

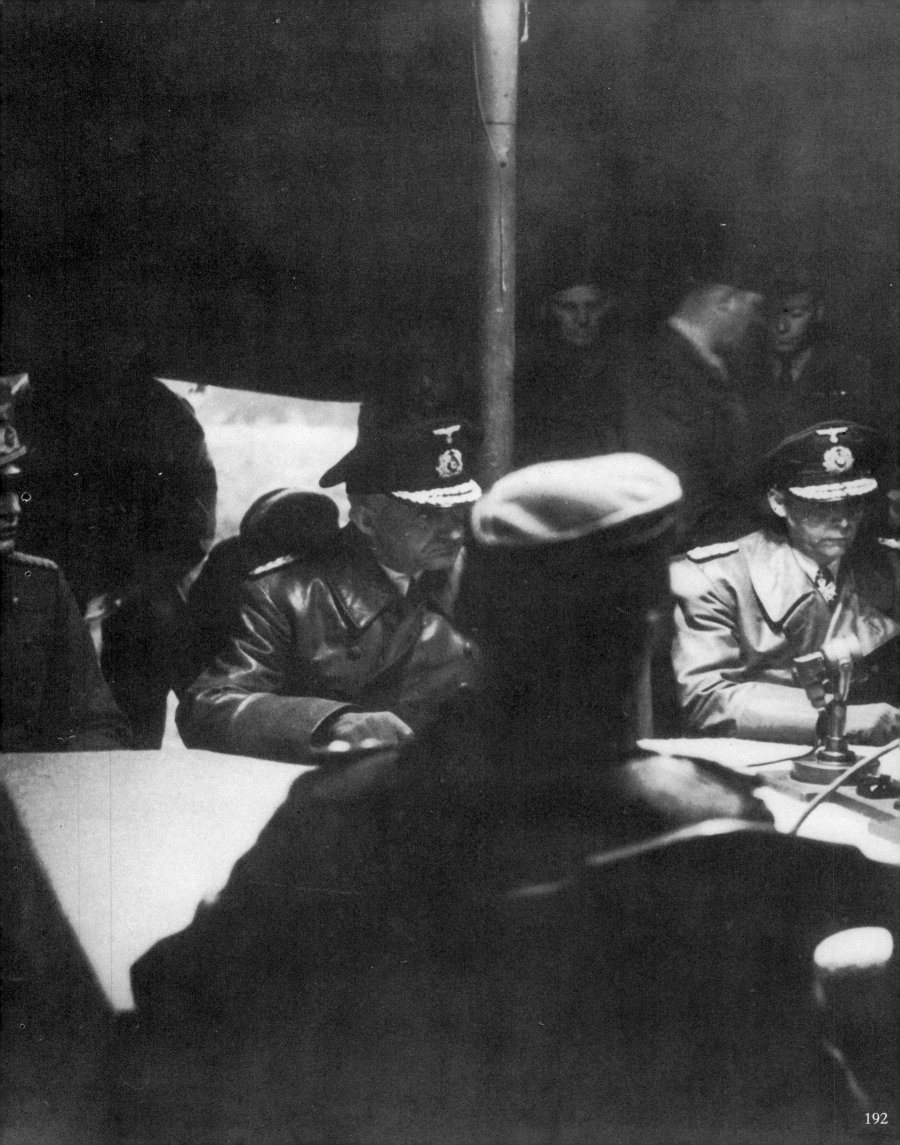

'Yesterday morning at 2.41 a.m. (May 7th, 1945) at Headquarters, General Jodl, the representative of the German High Command, and Grand Admiral Doenitz, the designated head of the German State, signed the act of unconditional surrender of all German land, sea, and air forces in Europe to the Allied Expeditionary Force, and simultaneously to the Soviet High Command. . .'

'Hostilities will end officially at one minute after midnight tonight (Tuesday, May 8th), but in the interests of saving lives the 'Cease Fire' began yesterday to be sounded all along the front. . .'

THE PRIME MINISTER'S BROADCAST
8th MAY, 1945

Field Marshal Montgomery reads the terms of surrender after the German capitulation on the British Front.

'This is your victory'

The Prime Minister spoke from the balcony of the
Ministry of Health building to the gathered crowds in Whitehall :

'God bless you all. This is your victory !

It is the victory of the cause of freedom in every land.

In all our long history we have never seen a

greater day than this. Everyone, man or woman, has done their best.

Everyone has tried. Neither the long years, nor the dangers,

nor the fierce attacks of the enemy, have in

any way weakened the independent resolve of the British nation.

GOD BLESS YOU ALL

May you long remain as citizens of a

great and splendid city. May you long remain as the

heart of the British Empire.'

8th MAY, 1945

London, V.E. Night.

'. . . and the war was over and the bells began to ring . .

198

Potsdam. July, 1945.

On July 26th, 1945, results of the General
Election declared a Conservative defeat.

'Just before dawn I awoke suddenly
with a sharp stab of almost physical pain.
A hitherto subconscious conviction that
we were beaten broke forth and dominated
my mind.'

'The decision of the British people has
been recorded in the votes counted today.
I have therefore laid down the charge
which was placed upon me in darker
times . . .'

'The final decision now lay in the main
with President Truman, who had the
weapon; but I never doubted what it
would be, nor have I ever doubted
since that he was right.'

TRIUMPH AND TRAGEDY,
'WAR MEMOIRS' VOL. VI.

Hiroshima, the first atom bomb, August 9th, 1945.

PEACE

'It fell to me in those days
to express the sentiments and resolves of the British nation
in that supreme crisis of its life.
That was to me an honour far beyond any dreams
or ambitions I had ever nursed; and it is one
that cannot be taken away.'

Victory Parade, 1946.

Holiday in Miami.

New York welcomes Mr. Churchill following his Fulton speech : ' An iron curtain has descended across the Continent.'

Berne, Switzerland, 1946, with his daughter, Miss Mary Churchill.   At Zurich he spoke of ' . . . a kind of United States of Europe ' to include ' a spiritually great Germany.'

Dover Castle, August 14th, 1946.

The Lord Warden of the Cinque Ports. ►

Paris, the Court of Honour in the Invalides. The award of the Medaille Militaire by the French Prime Minister, M. Paul Ramadier. May 10th, 1947.

'Be on your guard! I am going to speak in French
—a formidable undertaking and one which will put great
demands upon your friendship for Great Britain.'

St. Margaret's Westminster, 1947. The wedding of Miss Mary Churchill and Captain Christopher Soames.

The christening of Mr. Churchill's fifth grandchild, Arthur Nicholas Winston Soames, March 28th, 1948. ▶

The Congress of Europe.

The Hague, May 7th, 1948.

◀ Oslo. A visit to the Parliament
  of Norway, May 14th, 1948.

London. Birthday Portrait, 1951.

With his horse, Colonist II. 'Don't give your son money. As far as you can afford it, give him horses.'

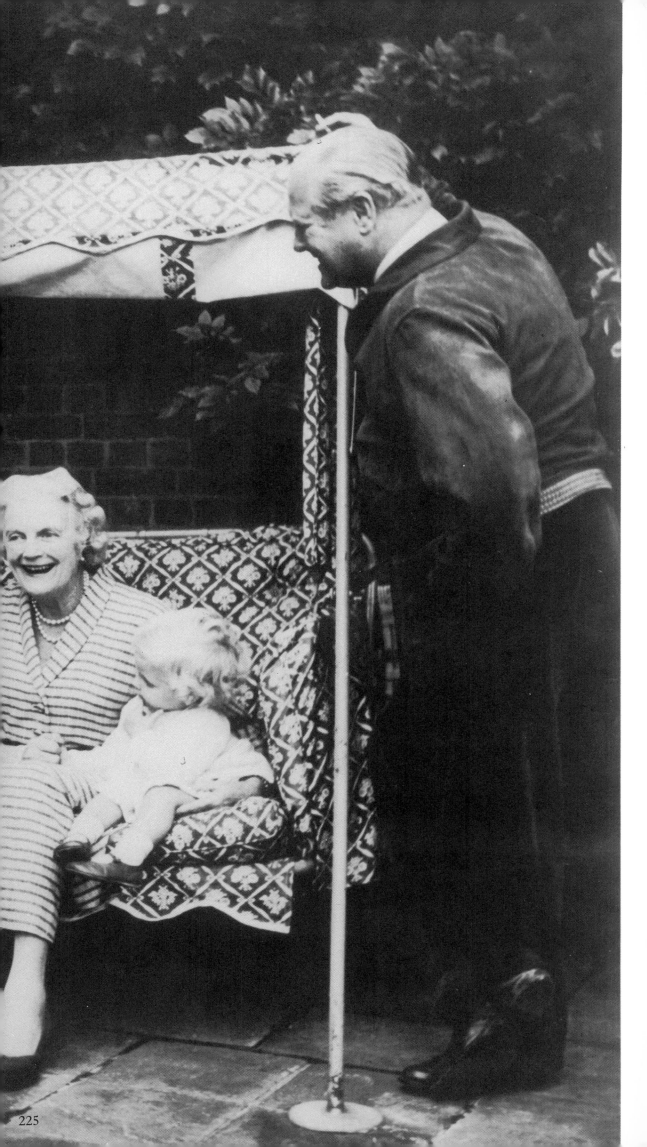

The Pink Terrace, Chartwell, 1951.

The Festival of Britain, May 4th, 1951.

' I am a child of the House of Commons. I was brought up in my father's house to believe in democracy.' On October 26th, 1951, Mr. Churchill once again became Prime Minister of Great Britain, at the age of seventy-six. The Churchill Arch in the new House of Commons.

THE KING IS DEAD . . . The Lying in State, Westminster Hall, 1952.

The Prime Minister leaves Buckingham Palace for the Coronation
of Her Majesty, Queen Elizabeth II, June 2nd, 1953.

LONG LIVE THE QUEEN.

ELIZABETHAN

'Queen Elizabeth II comes to the throne

at a time when a tormented mankind

stands uncertainly poised between world catastrophe

and a golden age. That it should be a golden age

of art and letters we can only hope—

science and machinery have their tales to tell—

but it is certain that if a true and lasting peace

can be achieved and if the nations will only let each other alone

an immense and undreamed of prosperity

with culture and leisure ever more widely spread can come,

perhaps even easily and swiftly,

to the masses of the people in every land.'

SIR WINSTON CHURCHILL

The drive to Westminster Abbey.

The Coronation of Elizabeth II.

Knight of the Garter.

St. George's Chapel,
Windsor Castle.

The guest of President Eisenhower, the White House, June 28th, 1954.

Number 10, Downing Street, 1954.

The Chancellor, Bristol University.

240

Westerham, Kent. Sir Winston with his grandson, Nicholas Soames.

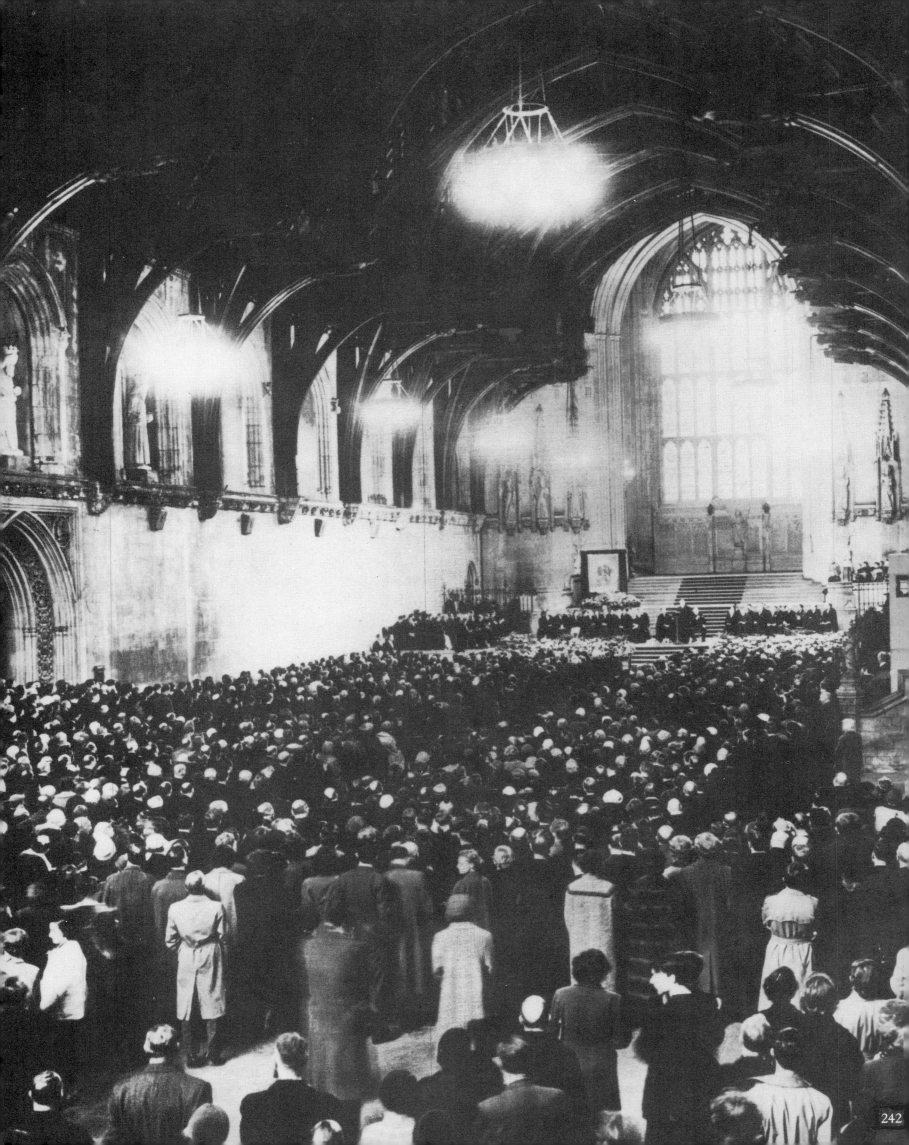

The Prime Minister's eightieth birthday. The presentation, Westminster Hall, of the portrait
painted by Mr. Graham Sutherland, a gift from both Houses of Parliament. November 30th, 1954.

244

Buckingham Palace. The Queen
with her Prime Ministers, 1955.

Her Majesty the Queen dined at
Number 10 Downing Street on the evening
before Sir Winston retired as
Prime Minister, April 4th, 1955.

He leaves 10 Downing Street for the last time as Prime Minister after his retirement, April 6th, 1955.

'I am perhaps the only man who has passed
through both the two supreme cataclysms of recorded history
in high executive office . . . These years of action and advocacy
comprise and express my life-effort, and I am content
to be judged upon them.'